LIFE FILES

DRUGS

JULIAN COHEN

Evans

EVANS BROTHERS LIMITED

Evans Brothers LImited
2A Portman Mansions
Chiltern Street
London W1M 1LE

First published 1996

British Library Cataloguing in
Publication Data. A catalogue
record for this book is available
from the British Library.

0 237 51508 3

ACKNOWLEDGEMENTS

Cover James King-Holmes
page 7 Tordai, The Hutchison Library **page 8**
Sheila Terry, Science Photo Library **page 9**
Topham Picture Point **page 11** The Hutchison
Library **page 13** James Prince, Science Photo
Library **page 14** Paul Brawn, Rex Features
page 16 Topham Picture Point **page 17** David
White, Rex Features **page 19** Rogan Coles/Link
page 21 Rex Features **page 24** Lori Adamski
Peek, Tony Stone Worldwide **page 25** Associated
Press, Topham Picture Point **page 28** BSIP,
Alexandre, Science Photo Library **page 29** Bruce
Coleman Limited **page 31** Rex Features **page
32** Topham Picture Point **page 35** Alexander
Isiaras, Science Photo Library **page 37** Topham
Picture Point **page 38** Rex Features **page 39**
Rex Features **page 41** Rasmussen, Rex Features
page 43 Gary Parker, Science Photo Library
page 45 Jeremy Young, Rex Features **page 48**
David Young Wolff, Tony Stone Worldwide **page
53** The Times, Rex Features

CONTENTS

More young people are using drugs. They start using drugs at a younger age and a wide range of drugs - legal and illegal - are available.

Drugs has been specially written for young people. It covers some of the most important issues surrounding young people's use of drugs today. In the past there has been a tendency to over-simplify the drugs problem. This book does not just give information about different drugs and tell you not to use drugs. It recognises that the drugs issue is very complex and focuses on a number of key questions that young people can consider. You need to reach your own informed conclusions about the drugs issue. I hope that today's young people will go on to make a better job of tackling the drug problem in future than we adults have been able to do so far. There is certainly plenty of room for improvement.

You can read through **Drugs** by yourself. However, the complexities of the issues involved mean you will benefit from talking with other people - other young people, your teachers and parents in particular. Each chapter focuses on a particular question and suggests some things for you to think about and discuss with other people.

Chapter 9 suggests some activities you might become involved in to help tackle the drugs issue (see page 54).

If you need information about different drugs look at pages 55-58. If you want to find out more about drugs look at the listings of organisations on page 59 and other books on page 60.

I would welcome your views about what you think of **Drugs**. You can write to me at Evans Brothers, 2A Portman Mansions, Chiltern Street, London W1M 1LE.

Julian Cohen

WHAT DO WE MEAN BY 'DRUGS'?

Chapter 1

What images come into your head when you think of 'drugs'? Many people immediately think of substances like heroin and cocaine. Other people might think of medicines and hospitals. Some people say that alcohol, the nicotine in tobacco and the caffeine in tea and coffee and some soft drinks are drugs. Yet many people who drink alcohol, smoke cigarettes or drink tea and coffee would be very

surprised, even angry, if they were told they were drug takers.

If you look up the word 'drug' in a dictionary you will probably find that one of the definitions focuses on medicines. An example is 'Any chemical substance which is used to prevent or cure disease'. In this book we are mainly concerned with drugs that are used non-medically, although

there is some overlap between the medical and non-medical use of drugs. The drugs in this book are described in detail on pages 55-58.

Books about non-medical drugs use different definitions. A common

Question

Do you drink alcohol or smoke cigarettes? If so, do you think of yourself as a drug taker?

About one third of young people aged 13 to 16 drink alcohol at least once a week. Does this mean they are drug takers?

"All in the mind?"

In some experiments, people have become 'drunk' drinking water when told it was gin. Some people have become 'stoned' when smoking a substance that has no physical effect but which they were told was cannabis.

definition is:
'A drug is any chemical substance that can be used to alter perception, mood or other psychological states'. In other words non-medical drugs are substances that can change the way people feel about themselves and the world around them.

'HARD' DRUGS AND 'SOFT' DRUGS

People often divide drugs into 'hard' drugs and 'soft' drugs or sometimes 'good'

Question
Chocolate and other foods can change the way you feel. Are they drugs?

drugs and 'bad' drugs. Heroin is usually seen as a hard drug. It is regarded as very dangerous. Many people use heroin illegally in dangerous quantities and ways, but it can be used safely - doctors prescribe heroin as a powerful painkiller for people with cancer. Alcohol is seen as a soft drug and relatively safe to use, yet alcohol can lead to alcoholism, driving accidents, violent behaviour and damage

Question
'Drugs may be good or bad, and whether they are seen as good or bad depends on who is looking at them.'
A. Weil and W. Rosen
'From Chocolate to Morphine' 1993.
Do you agree?

to the liver. The dangers of drug use are not just about the drugs themselves but how they are used (see chapter 4).

One interesting definition of drugs is 'Drugs is something other people do.'

More than 20 per cent of 15 year olds smoke every day. How does this young man's smoking affect other people's health as well as his own?

We all have a tendency to think of the drugs we use ourselves as 'good' and may not even see them as drugs at all. We are often quick to damn the drugs used by other people.

What society sees as good and bad drugs changes over time. For many years cigarettes were seen as useful drugs which could help people relax and which had few problems associated with them. In the 1950s and 60s cigarette adverts often featured famous sportsmen. We now think very differently about cigarettes. We know that they damage the lungs and can kill. Cigarette advertising is banned on television and cigarette packets carry a health warning.

In the 19th century opium-based drugs like laudanum (which has similarities to heroin) were widely used in the U.K. in beers, and in potions given to children to make them sleep. Many famous people took opium,

Coca Cola was first introduced in America in 1885 as a 'valuable brain tonic and cure for all nervous afflictions'. It contained caffeine and cocaine. In 1906 the company was forced to remove the cocaine. Today Coca Cola is sold with caffeine or caffeine free.

including Florence Nightingale, poets such as Byron and Keats, and politicians such as Gladstone. Thomas de Quincey describes his experiences, including the severe physical and mental suffering, in **Confessions of an English Opium-eater** (published 1821). Cannabis was used as a herbal remedy for a range of ailments. Even Queen Victoria is alleged to have been prescribed cannabis by her doctor. We have only had laws regulating drug use in this country since the 1920s. What is regarded as acceptable changes over time. The reasons for these changes are very complex and involve issues such as economics, developments in medical knowledge, which sort of people use drugs and how their associated lifestyle is viewed by others.

> 66 Every part of the earth that is capable of producing drugs has been used for this purpose. Vast areas of Europe are covered by vines. The cannabis plant flourishes in Africa and Asia; and from the Middle East down through Asia the opium poppy grows - both in its wild state and under cultivation. In the cooler, wetter climate of the British Isles some of the best arable land in the country is turned over to the production of that most English narcotic, the hop. In the Americas there are plantations of the coca plant, tobacco and cactuses containing mescaline, and throughout the world there are mushrooms containing other hallucinogenic drugs. The only people with no traditional drug of their own would appear to be the Eskimos who live in a land so bleak and uncompromising that it does not permit the cultivation of any intoxicant. 99
>
> Michael Gossop *Living with Drugs* Ashgate 1993

DRUGS AROUND THE WORLD

Which drugs are acceptable and used also varies in different countries and cultures. In South American countries such as Colombia chewing coca (from which cocaine and crack are made) is common amongst agriculture workers to help them work long hours in the fields. In some Moslem countries there are very strict laws against the use of alcohol. Mormons are forbidden to take any drugs including tea and coffee. Many Afro-Carribeans regard cannabis as a herbal medicine. Rastafarians see cannabis as an important part of their religion and culture and yet many do not drink alcohol.

The 20th century has seen many technological developments in chemistry. This has led to more efficient processing of naturally-occurring drugs and a whole new range of man-made

Opium is made by drying the juice taken from poppy seed capsules.

drugs. Developments in transport have resulted in drugs being much more easily moved from one part of the world to another. The demand for and supply of drugs is now worldwide.

DRUG MISUSE AND ABUSE

The terms **misuse** and **abuse** are difficult to define precisely. **Drug misuse** usually refers to illegal drugs, such as heroin, cocaine, amphetamine, ecstasy, LSD and cannabis. But the term is also often used to describe use of drugs which are not illegal to use such as solvents (glue, gas, aerosols etc.), poppers (liquid gold, nitrites) or raw magic mushrooms. Strictly speaking the word 'misuse' suggests the drugs are being used in the wrong way and that used in another way, such as medicines prescribed by a doctor, they would be acceptable. This is confusing because many of the drugs mentioned do not have medical uses and many people would regard any use of them as misuse.

Drug abuse usually refers to drugs which are regarded as harmful to the user, and illegal drug use is often referred to as abuse no matter how much is taken and whether it produces harmful effects or not. Alcohol use is only sometimes referred to as abuse depending on the quantity taken. Taking solvents is always referred to as abuse. What is use and what is abuse is very much up to how people see the drugs issue. It is complicated by the fact that it is not just the illegal drugs which can cause problems for people.

ADDICTION AND DEPENDENCE

The word **addict** refers to someone who is so hooked on drugs that he or she takes them continuously and cannot stop. Many experts now prefer to use the term **dependence** because addiction has so many meanings for different people. Physical dependence is when someone has taken certain drugs (such as heroin or alcohol) on a regular basis and his or her body needs repeat doses to avoid withdrawal symptoms like shaking, sweating or vomiting. Psychological dependence can happen with any drug and is when someone needs to keep taking a drug to feel OK and able to face the world.

Attitudes towards drug dependence vary. We hear a lot about heroin dependence and to most people it is totally unacceptable. Dependence on alcohol (alcoholism) is very

Find out!
Find out about the use of drugs in different times, countries and cultures. Some useful books to help you do this are listed at the end of this book.

common but much more tolerated. Dependence on caffeine from tea and coffee drinking is usually not even seen as dependence at all.

DRUG CATEGORIES

Mood-altering drugs can be grouped into different categories depending on the effects they can have.(The law groups illegal drugs into class A, B and C, depending on how dangerous they are thought to be. See page 36.)

Depressant drugs slow down the activity of the brain and cause sleepiness and relief of anxiety. They include drugs derived from the opium poppy (codeine, morphine and heroin), synthetic heroin-like drugs (such as pethidine

and methadone) as well as alcohol, barbiturates and tranquillisers (such as valium and librium).

Stimulant drugs increase the activity of the brain and make people feel more energetic and awake. They include caffeine (in tea, coffee and some chocolate and soft drinks), nicotine (in tobacco), amphetamine, cocaine and crack (a form of cocaine) and ecstasy.

Hallucinogenic drugs distort people's senses so they see and hear the world differently. They may see and experience things which are not there. Hallucinogenic drugs include LSD and magic mushrooms.

Other drugs Some drugs, such as cannabis and solvents, do not fit easily into these three categories and tend to have a combination of effects.

Question
'If we were starting all over again tobacco and alcohol would be illegal to use.' What do you think?

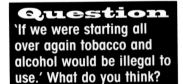

WHY DO YOUNG PEOPLE USE DRUGS?

The reasons that young people use drugs are many and varied. If you just read the tabloid newspapers you might think young people only use drugs because they are bored, pressured by friends or forced to use them by evil drug-pushers. In contrast, people who use drugs often say they get something positive and pleasurable from the experience. To really understand why someone uses drugs you need to take account of what it means to the user. The motivation for using drugs will be different for different people.

Reasons for drug use can have a lot to do with how people deal with their emotions. They may use drugs to feel better about themselves, to escape emotional upset, to feel less anxious, to avoid thinking about things or making decisions or to make them feel independent. There may also be more physical reasons such as blocking out physical pain and the pleasure of the 'buzz'. Drugs may also be used to increase or reduce energy levels or to help people relax.

Some motivations for drug use seem to have a lot

> 66 ...it is apparent that drug use in general is the outcome of interaction between the drug, the personal characteristics of the individual and the environment. Few people would suggest that either drug use in general or drug dependence are caused by any single factor. 99
>
> M. Plant *Drugs in Perspective* 1987

Smoking crack, a form of cocaine. The drug has a strong stimulant effect but may leave the user feeling lethargic and depressed.

to do with the users' relationships with other people. Using drugs may help some people feel accepted by others, make them feel less shy and lonely or make communication with people easier.

Other reasons for drug use may have more to do with the environment in which people live. If drugs are freely available and not too expensive the temptation to use will be greater. There may also be pressure to use from friends (peer pressure). Some people would add that many young people are tricked into drug use by drug dealers who give youngsters free drugs and get them quickly hooked.

To begin to better understand the reasons why people use drugs it is useful to consider the different ways in which they use. In particular, the reasons why people start using drugs in the first place may be very different to those influencing why they might carry on using or become dependent.

> 66 The demon drug-pusher as an alien figure waiting in the shadows to corrupt the nation's youth is a figment of the imagination. 99
>
> Drug Scenes *Royal College of Psychiatrists* 1987

Some people may take drugs to make them feel less shy and lonely.

EXPERIMENTING WITH DRUGS

This is where people use drugs for the first time. The reasons young people experiment with drugs include:

- **Availability and cost** – if drugs are freely available and cheap, the incentive to use is greater. Many drugs have become more easily available and prices have fallen. For example, drugs like cannabis, poppers (liquid gold), LSD and solvents (glue and gas) are quite cheap compared to the cost of alcohol.

- **Curiosity** – young people like to try out new experiences. That is part of growing up. For many young people the motivation for experimenting with drugs may be just to see what it is like.

- **Being bored** – for some young people trying drugs is something to do and provides a bit of excitement in an otherwise dull life.

- **Feeling grown up** – for some young people experimenting with drugs may be similar to the first drink of alcohol and make them feel they are now grown up.

- **As a protest** – for some young people drug use may seem all the more attractive if parents, teachers and other adults tell them not to do it.

- **Pressure from others** – if everyone else is doing it young people may feel left out if they don't. Some friends may pressurise them to use and make out they are 'chicken' if they don't.

Peer pressure is one of the main reasons given by many adults to explain young people's drug use. But what do we really mean by 'peer pressure', especially as it is nearly always used in a negative way to criticise young people? There is tremendous pressure not to use certain drugs amongst groups of young people. Peer pressure may be positive. It may be more appropriate to talk about peer support or peer preference. It is also interesting that people rarely use the idea of 'peer pressure' to explain adult behaviour, as though adults never respond to pressures from other adults.

These reasons for experimenting with drugs are very much part of being a young person and growing up. They do not indicate anything particularly abnormal. They are similar reasons to those used to explain other adolescent behaviour such as joining gangs, petty crime, responding to dares, riding motorbikes, staying up all night or wearing different styles of clothes.

RECREATIONAL USE OF DRUGS

This is where someone has moved beyond experimenting with drugs and starts to use them in a relatively regular but controlled way. The reasons people start using regularly in this way may be similar to the reasons they originally started using. However, it also often has to do with them feeling they get something particularly positive out of the drug experience. Additional reasons for recreational drug use may include:

- **Enhancing social activities** such as dancing and listening to music.

The drug ecstasy is popular with many young people at raves. It gives a 'rush' of energy and allows users to dance for hours. The after effects can be very unpleasant, and some young people have died after using ecstasy.

Find out!

Why do young people take drugs?'. Ask this question of some adults and young people. Are the reasons given by adults and young people the same?

Many adults think young people use drugs because they are pressurised by friends or dealers to do so.

The evidence suggests that most young people get drugs from friends and acquaintances and that rather than being 'pushed' the drugs are often 'pulled'. In other words there is clearly a demand for drugs amongst young people and many regard it as a favour if a friend offers to get them some.

- **Loss of inhibitions** so that communication and understanding is improved between people. This may include feeling more confident in sexual situations. (A number of studies have shown that young people are often under the influence of drugs - legal or illegal - when having sex).

- **A desire to explore different feelings** and ways of seeing and experiencing the world.

- **As a part of a fashion** that includes dress, music, social activity.

- **Enjoying the 'buzz'** and possibly experiencing it as more pleasant than alcohol.

- **Feeling it is a relatively cheap way to enjoy oneself.**

Question

'Drug use by young people is part and parcel of consumer society.' What do you think?

DEPENDENT USE OF DRUGS

Dependent use of drugs is where drugs are taken continually as an important aspect of getting through the day. It is often a more chaotic style of drug use where large quantities of drugs are taken and if the usual drug of choice is not available other drugs will be used. The dependent drug user may be high on drugs for most of their waking life. But the old saying 'once an addict, always an addict' is not true. Many people who are addicted to or dependent on drugs manage to 'kick the habit' in time.

For some people, drugs seem to offer a way out of problems such as unemployment or poor housing.

Drug dependence is very different from experimenting or recreational drug use and is relatively rare amongst the younger age range. It usually has more to do with the social and emotional problems people experience. The reasons for dependent drug use may include:

- **Blocking out unpleasant feelings or memories.**
  Drug use may shelter people from painful experiences in their past and in the present.

- **Blocking out physical pain.**

- **Providing a purpose and meaning in life.**
  Obtaining money for drugs, getting the drugs, avoiding the police and being part of a drug scene with other people all takes time and energy.

- **To give confidence** to face other people and difficult situations.

- **Helping to cope** with poverty, unemployment, bad housing and no prospects. Drug use can help people forget day-to-day worries.

There may be some overlap between the reasons for recreational drug use and dependent drug use.

People tend to use drugs in different ways for varying reasons that have to do with their feelings, situation and the wider society. There is no simple answer to the question of why people use drugs. This, together with the fact that many people have pleasurable experiences using drugs, means attempts to stop people using drugs may not always have the desired effect.

WHAT ARE THE TRENDS IN YOUNG PEOPLE'S DRUG USE?

It can sometimes appear from the media that most young people are using illegal drugs. Yet according to many teachers and parents, very few of the young people they know are involved with drugs. What is the truth about the trends in young people's drug use?

Over the last few years there have been many surveys of young people's drug use. Most of them are based on interviews and questionnaires. The problem arises as to whether people answer truthfully. They might exaggerate their use of drugs or they might wish to conceal it. Most of the

Recent research has found little difference in whether young people have used drugs, between deprived, inner city schools and more affluent schools in the leafy suburbs. They also find little difference in drug use between girls and boys and between black and white youngsters, although figures are lower for young people of Asian origin.

studies also only ask whether people have used certain drugs or not. They do not go into how often people use, how much they use, or how it affects them. Whilst these studies are very useful in helping to judge the trends, they can only provide limited information.

SMOKING AND DRINKNG

How many young people smoke and drink? Over 90 per cent of the UK adult population drink alcohol. About one third of 13 to16-year-olds drink alcohol at least once a week. Boys tend to drink more alcohol more often than girls but recently girls have been catching up with boys. Recent reports suggest the overall consumption of alcohol amongst young people might be declining and that this may be related to greater use of illegal and socially disapproved of drugs.

The number of adults who smoke has been falling. More men than women smoke, although again women have been catching up with men. Amongst young people surveys show about five per cent of 13-year-olds smoke at least one cigarette a week, rising to over 20 per cent being daily smokers by the age of 15. More young girls than boys smoke cigarettes and some people have argued that the only growth market for the cigarette companies in the developed world is now among young women.

ILLEGAL DRUGS

A recent study by Manchester University of 15 and 16-year-olds found that 47 per cent claimed to have used an illegal or socially disapproved of drug and more than two thirds claimed to have been in situations where drugs were on offer. The most used drug was cannabis, with cocaine and heroin least used.

Percentage having used each drug

- 41% cannabis
- 25% LSD
- 22% poppers/liquid gold
- 16% amphetamine
- 13% solvents
- 12% magic mushrooms
- 7% ecstasy
- 5% tranquillisers
- 4% cocaine or crack
- 3% heroin

Surveys show that more young people are experimenting with drugs compared to a few years ago. In some areas up to a half of 15 to16-year-olds may have tried an illegal drug at least once. Other studies show lower figures but most recent surveys show at least a quarter to a third of 16-year-olds have tried drugs (other than alcohol or tobacco) at least once. Many studies also show the numbers experimenting with drugs increase in the 16 to 20-year-old age group. Use of drugs, other than alcohol and cigarettes, is clearly becoming more common amongst young people.

The main illegal drug used is cannabis. The Institute for the Study of Drug Dependence has estimated that over a million people in the UK use cannabis each year and that many more, some who are now parents, will have used it when they were younger. In some communities the use of cannabis is almost 'normalised' and not regarded as deviant.

Whilst drugs such as heroin, cocaine and crack (a form of cocaine) are often in the headlines their use is relatively rare amongst younger age groups.

Cannabis is made from the dried flowers and leaves of the cannabis plant or from the resin of the plant. It is usually smoked, with or without tobacco. Users can feel more relaxed, but may become lethargic or paranoid. Regular smoking may damage the lungs, especially if it is mixed with tobacco.

Heroin use grew rapidly in the UK in the mid 1980s and although there are estimates of 100,000 heroin users today, the number of users does not seem to have greatly increased. In fact some people would argue that heroin use is now regarded as unfashionable by most young people, in contrast to many other drugs. Cocaine has been used in this country for many years but it is only recently that crack, a smokeable form of cocaine, has become more widely available. Despite the newspaper claims about a 'crack epidemic', still seems to be concentrated in certain inner city areas and its use has not become as widespread as predicted.

Sniffing solvents (glue, gas, aerosols etc) can give a quick 'high' of happy feelings, but the user can then feel sick, drowsy or hungover for a day. Each year, about 150 people die from using solvents (see page 28).

The average age of first use of drugs seems to be falling. This means that more young people are experimenting with drugs at the age of 11 or 12 than was the case a few years ago. This is hardly surprising if more teenagers are using drugs.

The use of solvents (glue, gas, aerosols etc) seems to be more common in younger age groups. There has also been a definite trend away from the use of glue to the use of more dangerous gasses and aerosols. The campaign to stop shopkeepers selling glue to youngsters has been partly blamed for increasing the use of gasses and aerosols. Where young people's access to alcohol is restricted, the use of solvents may increase.

CHANGES IN FASHION

Developments in technology and changes in fashion have also meant that new drugs constantly become available.

Although ecstasy has been around since the turn of the century it was only in 1988 that it began to be used in clubs in the UK. Recent estimates have suggested there may be as many as 500,000 regular ecstasy users in the UK. Drugs such as MDA (an ecstasy-type drug), ketamine (used as an anaesthetic on animals) and GHB (also an anaesthetic-type drug) have recently been used in clubs in this country for the first time. Drugs come into and go out of fashion quite quickly and it looks as though this will continue into the rest of the 1990s with new 'designer drugs' coming on to the market.

LSD, which is usually dropped on to paper squares, has recently come back into fashion. LSD is a hallucinogen, which causes people to see and hear things differently.

" Some experts suggest that there may be five times as many people dependent on heroin as seek out help, meaning there may be more than 100,000 such people in the UK. "

There has been an increase in the use of anabolic steroids in the 1990s. They are often used by sports people and body builders in an attempt to increase muscle and performance. Many regular steroid users inject their drugs. Steroid use has also become more fashionable on the club scene, where people use them to help get the 'perfect body' and stand out on the dance floor.

A further trend emerges when the patterns of drug use between young males and females are examined. Surveys carried out before the middle 1980s always showed a lot more boys than girls involved with drugs. Those conducted more recently have often shown little difference in the numbers experimenting with drugs. Some studies have even shown girls of 15 to 16 to be more likely to have used illegal drugs than boys of the same age. This may have something to do with the way the drug scene has focused on clubs and pubs. Fifteen to16-year-old girls often look older and find it relatively easy to get into pubs and clubs compared to boys. Girls may also mix with boys who are much older and have easier access to drugs.

Many body builders use anabolic steriods to increase muscle size.

AT HOME AND ABROAD

Drug use amongst young people has also increased in other developed countries. However, there may be differences in which drugs are used and in what ways. Solvent use by young people is almost unheard of in the Netherlands. Cocaine and crack use is far greater in America than in any other developed country. A drug called PCP has been used in America for many years but is rarely available in Europe. For a long time Sweden had a much bigger problem with amphetamines being injected than heroin. With the break-up of the Communist block and the opening of borders, reports suggest that drug use amongst young people has greatly increased in East European countries. The increase in young people's drug use is an international phenomenon.

There may also be differences in the extent of drug use within different cultures in

This American couple are dependent on crack. Crack use has become wide-spread in America, especially in deprived, inner city areas. Its use has grown in the UK, but not to anywhere near the same extent as in the USA.

the UK. Despite the stereotypes about heavy drug use amongst people of Afro-Caribbean origin, recent surveys show very few differences in rates of drug use amongst black and white youngsters. There may be less drug use amongst young people of Asian origin but this seems to be increasing and catching up with white youngsters.

Many young people grow out of the use of illegal and socially disapproved of drugs in time. Getting a job, having a family, and all the responsibilities that go with it, result in most people reverting to more acceptable legal drugs, especially alcohol. With the current long-term recession and popularity of drugs amongst young people it may be that more will use illegal drugs for longer than has been the situation in the past.

Find out!
Interview some adults about their 'drug careers' - which drugs, if any, they have used, when, how much, to what effect etc. If you cannot broach the subject of illegal drugs, ask about alcohol and cigarettes.

Find out!
Find out about patterns of drug use in your locality. You could contact local Drug Advice and Information Agencies and ask them about any local surveys that have been carried out. You might ask the staff for their impressions of what is going on locally. You could also ask young people about their impressions of the local scene.

HOW DANGEROUS IS DRUG USE?

Some adults seem to think that every young person who uses drugs will end up dead. Many young people believe drug use, especially use of drugs like cannabis, is not very dangerous at all. The truth lies somewhere between these two extremes. Drug use can never be 100 per cent safe. There are always risks, but it is not always as dangerous as some people make out.

You can find detailed information about the effects and dangers of drugs on pages 55 to 58 of this book. Understanding the real dangers of drug use is complicated. Dangers vary with the use of different drugs and how they are taken but account needs to be taken of the person who is using the drug (the SET) and where the drug is taken (the SETTING).

> 66 In the UK each year over 100,000 people die prematurely from the effects of smoking cigarettes. About 20-30,000 deaths are alcohol-related through illness and accidents. 99

> 66 The vast majority of people who use drugs come to no harm, and many will feel that they have benefitted...from the relaxation, diversion or temporarily improved social, intellectual or physical performance that can be afforded by some drugs. But there are very serious risks. 99
> Institute for the Study of Drug Dependence
> *Drug Abuse Briefing 1994*

THE DRUG TAKEN

Different drugs carry different risks. Regular use of depressant drugs like heroin, alcohol or tranquillisers can lead to physical dependence, where withdrawal symptoms are experienced if the user does not have repeat doses. Taking too much of these drugs can also lead to an overdose, a coma and possible death. This does not happen with drugs like cannabis or LSD. Stimulant drugs which give a rush of energy (such as amphetamine, cocaine and ecstasy) can be particularly dangerous to people who have heart or blood pressure problems. Hallucinogenic drugs like LSD and magic mushrooms (and to some extent large doses of

Question
Is society turning a blind eye to the problems associated with alcohol and cigarettes compared with other drugs?

cannabis and ecstasy) change people's perceptions of the world and can lead them to do dangerous things.

The risks of taking a drug also depend on:

• How much is taken. Obviously the greater the amount taken the greater the risk.

• How often it is taken. If a drug is taken more often the dangers increase. With some drugs people develop a tolerance to the effects, which means they have to take more of the drug, more often, to get the same effect.

• What else might be mixed with the drug. Some illegal drugs such as heroin, cocaine, amphetamine and ecstasy may be mixed with other substances, which may themselves be dangerous.

• Whether different drugs are being taken together. Taking an illegal drug whilst drinking alcohol is very common. The effects of combining drugs are often difficult to predict and result in increased danger.

• How the drug is taken. Injecting drugs is particularly dangerous. The dose is taken in one go so the risk of overdose is increased. Injecting can lead to dangerous infections. If injecting equipment is shared between people there is a real danger of passing on infections like hepatitis or HIV (the virus that leads to AIDS). More than 2,500 people in the UK have contracted HIV in this way and many have developed AIDS and died. About 150 mainly young people die a year from using solvents, most of them from squirting aerosols or gases straight down the throat, which freezes the airways. Putting solvents in a large bag and then placing the bag over the head has led to death through suffocation.

> **66** Some 'ecstasy' tablets have been found to be dog worming tablets and tropical fish tank cleaners. It is impossible to tell what is in a tablet just by looking at it. **99**

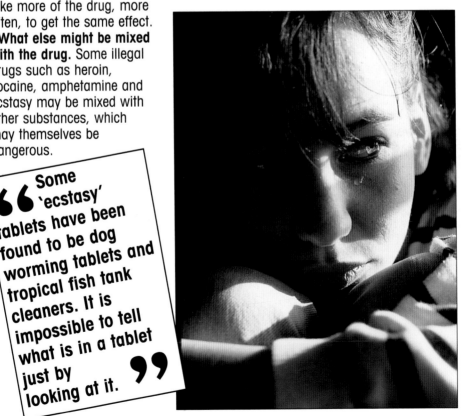

People usually take drugs to try to make them feel better. But if someone is depressed, drugs can often make them feel even worse.

THE SET

The dangers of drug use also vary depending on the person who is using the drugs. The set can depend on, among other things:

• **The mood of the person.** If someone is depressed or anxious when taking drugs it often makes them feel even worse. If they take hallucinogenic drugs like LSD or magic mushrooms or a strong dose of cannabis or ecstasy they might feel really disturbed and do dangerous things.

• **The expectations** of what is going to happen. Many first-time users may not know about how the drug might affect them. This may mean they have an unpleasant experience, not know what to do and get into problems.

• **Physical health.** If someone has heart or blood pressure problems, epilepsy, liver problems, diabetes or asthma, use of drugs may be particularly dangerous.

• **Body weight.** The effects and dangers of drugs are greater for someone who is lighter.

People with eating disorders like anorexia or bulimia may also find use of drugs makes their condition worse.

The dangers of drug use may also be different for males and females. In most situations the same amount of a drug will have a greater effect on a woman than on a man. This may be because males and females have a different physical make-up and their bodies deal differently with drugs. Drugs may also affect women's menstrual cycles and the effectiveness of contraceptives. If a woman is pregnant, drug use may affect her baby.

THE SETTING

Where people use drugs and what they are doing at the time can also affect the risks involved.

Most young people do not have their own homes where they can take drugs. Some take drugs in dangerous, lonely places like

Question
How do the risks of drug use compare with the risks of other potentially dangerous activities such as boxing and some outdoor pursuits?

Using drugs in lonely places can add to the dangers of the drugs themselves.

canal or river banks, near railway lines or roads, on wasteland or in derelict buildings. Accidents are more likely in such places, and if anything does go wrong it is unlikely help will be near or an ambulance can be easily called.

The dangers of driving whilst under the influence of alcohol are well known, but it is just as dangerous to drive, cycle or operate machinery having taken other drugs.

Many young people say they have sexual intercourse whilst under the influence of drugs - particularly alcohol and cannabis. Being high on drugs can make it more difficult to stay in control - to say no and to practise safer sex. Unwanted pregnancy and catching sexually transmitted diseases, including HIV, become more likely.

The dangers of using ecstasy in crowded, hot clubs have been reported in the press. Ecstasy gives a boost of energy and has been used for non-stop all-night dancing. Doing this in a hot, crowded club has led to young people becoming dehydrated and getting heat exhaustion. Over the last few years about 50 young people have died like this. Having a break from dancing ('chilling out'), cooling off and drinking plenty of water to replace lost fluids (not alcohol, as it dehydrates people more) can reduce the risks of overheating.

Where young people use drugs may also have a bearing on the likelihood of them being caught with an illegal drug. Being charged with an offence and being convicted leads to a criminal record. This can be very disturbing for the young person and their

Question

Some people seem to get into drug problems more easily than others. Why do you think this is so?

family. It can also mean they will be barred from certain jobs, especially jobs involving working with children or young people, and may prevent them obtaining a visa to the USA. Being involved with drug use in school or college may result in being expelled and damaging future qualifications and opportunities (see chapter 8).

CONCLUSION

It is difficult to predict the effects and risks of drug use for different people. What may be relatively safe for one person might be dangerous for someone else. What may be relatively safe in one situation might be particularly dangerous in another situation. The dangers of drug use are very real but also very complicated. To understand the dangers the drug, set and setting factors all need to be taken into account.

Find out!

Many young people seem to think cannabis is a very safe drug, but there are risks. Work out what some of the dangers of using cannabis might be. Take into account set and setting factors and the likely ways young people may use cannabis.

DOES DRUGS EDUCATION WORK?

Over the last few years there have been a host of drug education and information programmes and campaigns targeted at young people in an attempt to stop them using drugs. The main message has been that drugs are dangerous and can kill and that the best thing to do is to 'Say No' to drugs. Yet more and more people have been using drugs. Something is clearly going wrong.

DIFFERENT TYPES OF DRUG EDUCATION

Approaches to drugs education have changed over the last 20 years. The main ones, roughly in order of appearance, have been:

1. The 'shock/ scare' approach where young people are told of the horrors of using drugs with graphic images such as dead heroin addicts in a mortuary.

2. The 'information' approach where young people are given the facts about drugs (and especially the dangers) on the assumption that if the facts are known drugs will not be used.

An anti-drugs poster from the 1990s

3. The 'attitudes/ values' approach with a focus on a drug-free lifestyle. This approach often uses famous people, on the understanding that young people will want to be like their heroes or heroines.

4. The 'refusal skills' approach where young people learn how to 'Say No' to drugs.

5. The 'alternative highs' approach where an attempt is made to replace the highs and excitement of drug use with other forms of risk-taking such as rock climbing, pot-holing, abseiling etc.

6. The 'self esteem' approach where it is assumed that young people of low self-esteem are more likely to take drugs and that if they can be made to feel better about themselves they will not need to use drugs.

7. The 'peer education' approach where it is assumed young people are more likely to listen to other young people rather than adults. This might involve young people leading sessions or performing plays for other young people.

Most developed countries have drug information and education programmes targeted at young people. Apart from the UK, America, Australia and the Netherlands have probably done most work in this area. The Americans have used high-profile 'Just Say No' campaigns, with famous personalities endorsing drug-free lifestyles. The Netherlands approach tends to be more low key, avoiding the 'shock/horror' approach and high-profile media coverage. The approach in the UK and in Australia is somewhere between these two.

An anti-drugs poster in India

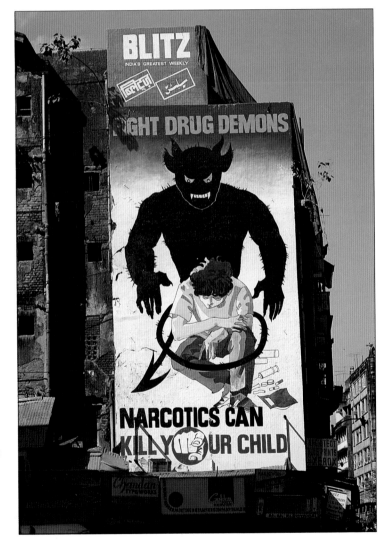

Chapter 5

THE IMPACT OF DRUGS EDUCATION ON YOUNG PEOPLE

The largest and most scientific evaluation of school-based drugs education in the UK was carried out in Scotland. It found that levels of knowledge about drugs were raised among pupils but there was no impact on their attitudes to drugs or on their reported use of illegal drugs, alcohol, tobacco or solvents. The report suggested that teachers need to:
- be credible sources of information
- avoid stereotypes
- encourage young people to make their own decisions
- provide information to reduce the harm from drug use.

This and other reports suggest that drugs education programmes of all kinds do not seem to stop young people using drugs, even though knowledge of drugs may be increased.

All this does not mean there is no point in drugs education. Education has an important role in reducing the harm that young drug users can do to themselves. But the information must be carefully presented. Many drugs information and education programmes exaggerate the dangers of drug use. Some may

Question
'The aim of stopping young people taking drugs may be inappropriate where so many young people are using drugs. Education which enables young people to understand drugs and avoid the harms may be more relevant.' (from a report on drug education in Scotland) What do you think?

> **The accent on danger has aroused first the curiosity and then the contempt of many young people. They feel drugs have been ludicrously presented as all equally menacing. Many young people despise the notion that one thing will lead to another, seeing it as evidence of how little their parents and authority understand about drugs.**
>
> Andrew Cragg *Druglink* 1994

> **Available evidence supports the simple conclusion that providing young people, or others, with information on alcohol, drugs or other health-related issues, does not necessarily (or even probably) lead to behaviour change. Moreover, the use of fear-arousal or 'horror film' approaches is clearly unproductive and should at all costs be avoided.**
>
> M. Plant and M. Plant
> *Risk-Takers – Alcohol, Drugs, Sex and Youth* 1992

even end up lying about drugs. Young people may find, through friends or their own experiments with drugs, that it is not that dangerous and then mistrust people who say it is.

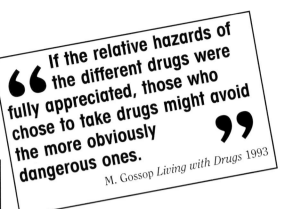

" If the relative hazards of the different drugs were fully appreciated, those who chose to take drugs might avoid the more obviously dangerous ones. **"**

M. Gossop *Living with Drugs* 1993

WHAT IS TO BE DONE?

There is a real dilemma about the future of drugs education and information in this country. Most teachers, parents and politicians strongly support the aim of stopping young people taking drugs. This is called primary prevention. Yet we have a situation where more young people are experimenting with drugs and are ignoring the anti-drug message.

The alternative is to develop drugs education and information which is focused on reducing harm from drug use rather than aiming to stop use altogether. This approach is called harm reduction. It involves:

1. Accurate and relevant information about drugs which acknowledges the benefits as well as the risks of drug use.
2. Information about the law, where to get help if you need it etc.
3. Exploration of attitudes towards drug use, recognising that it is a complex issue and that there are many different views.

4. Developing skills (such as decision-making, assessing risks, communicating with others, helping others, how to get help when needed) on the understanding that young people make their own decisions about drug use despite what adults say.

This form of education is more 'about drugs' than 'against drugs' and aims to enable young people to make sensible, informed decisions about their own and other people's drug use, be it legal or illegal drugs.

To many adults this is very controversial and goes against their belief in primary prevention. They say that harm reduction condones drug use and that the only choice is to condemn drug use. People who advocate harm reduction education say they find the 'condone/ condemn' argument unhelpful in that drugs are here and being used and we have to face up to this reality.

Question
'If you do not condemn all drug use you are condoning it.' What do you think?

HOW MUCH CRIME IS LINKED TO DRUGS?

Drugs and criminal behaviour are linked in a number of ways:

Recent reports in the press have suggested that people who are addicted to heroin steal 2 billion pounds worth of goods each year and account for half of all property thefts in the UK. Dealers and police officers have been killed in drug raids. Drug-related crime has also been on the increase in many other countries. In what ways are drugs and crime related and how much crime can be attributed to drug use?

• People who use or supply illegal drugs.

• People who commit crimes such as theft, burglary, fraud, shoplifting to get goods they can trade for money to buy drugs.

• People who become violent and commit criminal offences whilst under the influence of drugs.

• Violence amongst drug dealers who may clash with rival gangs and dealers or be violent towards drug users who owe them money.

• Alcohol and drug-related driving offences

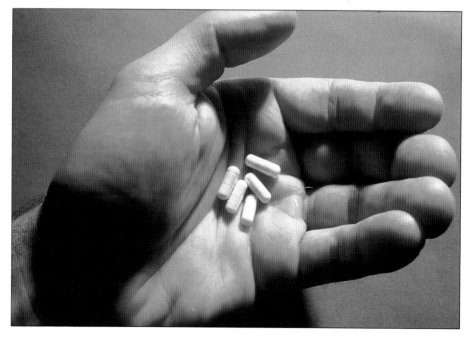

In the UK, supplying certain drugs carries a maximum penalty of life imprisonment.

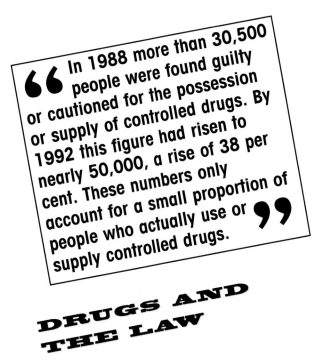

" In 1988 more than 30,500 people were found guilty or cautioned for the possession or supply of controlled drugs. By 1992 this figure had risen to nearly 50,000, a rise of 38 per cent. These numbers only account for a small proportion of people who actually use or supply controlled drugs. "

DRUGS AND THE LAW

The main law covering the use of drugs in the UK is called the Misuse of Drugs Act. It divides drugs into three groups depending on how dangerous they are thought to be. These include:

Class A drugs: cocaine and crack, ecstasy, heroin, LSD, methadone (a synthetic heroin type drug), opium, processed magic mushrooms and any Class B drug which is injected.

Class B drugs: amphetamine, barbiturates, cannabis and codeine.

Class C drugs: mild amphetamines, tranquillisers.

Offences can include:

• Possession for personal use.
• Possession with intent to supply.
• Supplying or offering to supply someone else.
• Production, cultivation or manufacture.

• Allowing premises you own or control to be used for the consumption or supply of certain drugs.

It is not illegal to be in possession of drugs such as amphetamines, cocaine, heroin or methadone if the person concerned has obtained them on prescription.

Maximum possible prison sentences are:

	Possession	Supplying
Class A drug	7 years	Life
Class B drug	5 years	14 years
Class C drug	2 years	5 years

Offenders sent to prison may also be fined.

The majority of drug offenders are aged 17 to 24 and mostly men. In most cases offences are concerned with the use of cannabis. In 1992, 85 per cent of offences were for possession or supply of cannabis, 12 per cent involved amphetamine, three per cent involved ecstasy, LSD or heroin and only two per cent involved cocaine or crack. (The total figure comes to over 100 per cent because some people were found guilty of offences involving more than one drug.)

Offenders found guilty of supplying drugs are often sent to prison and may also be fined. Those caught with small amounts of drugs (especially cannabis) for personal use are more likely to receive a fine or caution. Cautioning has become much more common. However, what happens to young people caught with illegal drugs can vary between different areas of the UK. Some police forces and some courts take a harder line than others.

A caution means that the offender does not go to court. It does not count as a criminal record. If someone is fined in a court for possession of a small amount of a drug like cannabis it does count as a criminal record. This may bar them from

A teenager has been arrested for a drug offence and is waiting at the police station for his parents to arrive.

future jobs, especially those which involve working with children.

The fact that many police forces now focus on supply rather than possession of drugs has sometimes meant more young people are being convicted for supplying drugs. For example, if a group of young people pool their money and one of them buys some drugs for the group, that person could be prosecuted for supplying drugs even if relatively small quantities were involved.

PAYING FOR THE HABIT

A dependent heroin user may need up to a gram of heroin a day and that will cost about £80. This works out at £29,200 a year. To make this amount of money from theft and burglary police suggest multiplying by three - on the basis that stolen goods will fetch about one third of their normal value.

It is clear that much crime is associated with people who need money to obtain drugs but the extent of such crime may sometimes be exaggerated. A lot of 'acquisitive' crime (theft, burglary, shoplifting etc) has to do with poverty – people steal in order to feed, clothe and house themselves and their families. Heroin users are often involved in crime before using drugs, and often unemployed and living in poverty. Others may have a job or have some other form of income or have a prescription for substitute drugs from a doctor.

Whatever the truth behind the statistics may be, drug-related crime creates serious problems for the victims. For this reason a number of senior police officers have recently suggested that most drugs should be 'decriminalised' so it is not an offence to use them and that users should obtain their drugs through health services rather than the black market. This is seen by some people as a way to cut crime at a stroke. For other people it is the last thing they wish to see happen.

DRUGS AND VIOLENCE

The black market in drugs and the large sums of money involved have resulted in many violent incidents. These have included clashes between rival gangs over territories, violence against users and dealers who owe money, and clashes with the police. There has been an increase in the number of drug-related incidents involving guns and a number of people have been killed, although this has not reached anything like the scale of the situation in some other countries. In America, drug-related violence has led to the deaths of thousands of people, including police officers. In South America, the cocaine trade has led to open battles between rival armies and many assassinations. In Italy, a number of deaths have been linked to Mafia control of drug supplies. Much more common in the UK are alcohol-related violence and

> 66 You can hear the guns going off every night in the South Bronx and Harlem; everyone knows someone who was killed in this battle. New York City will have over 2000 murders this year – perhaps half of them drug-related. 99
>
> Ernest Drucker *US drug policy* 1992

In the USA, two men are arrested for buying drugs. Penalties tend to be harsher in the USA than in this country.

Hundreds of people die and thousands are injured every year in road accidents where a driver has drunk alcohol.

disorder. Studies suggest that many violent assaults, murders and rapes are committed by people who are drunk. For example a 1989 British Medical Association report suggested that alcohol use was associated with 60 to 70 per cent of murders and manslaughters, 75 per cent of stabbings and half of the domestic assaults. A lot of violence against women is committed by men who are drunk and American research has suggested that alcohol use is often associated with sexual abuse of children. In comparison, users of illegal drugs tend not to be as violent as people who are drunk, although use of cocaine and crack, solvents and steroids has been connected with violent behaviour.

DRUNKENNESS OFFENCES

In 1990 over 86,000 people in the UK were found guilty or cautioned of the offence of drunkenness. This figure has remained relatively constant for a number of years. Again it mostly involves men. Of the 1990 figure, only 8 per cent were women.

DRIVING OFFENCES

Alcohol is implicated in many cases of dangerous driving, road traffic accidents and deaths. In 1992 about 700 people were killed in road traffic accidents where the driver had been drinking alcohol. Another 4,000

Question
The legal limit for drinking and driving is about two and a half pints of beer for the average-sized man. Some people argue the legal limit should be no alcohol at all. What do you think?

people were seriously injured. Forty per cent of drivers aged 20 to 24 killed on the roads are over the legal limit for alcohol. We do not know how many road traffic accidents involve other drugs but we do know that being under the influence of most drugs can impair driving ability.

CONCLUSION

In 1987 the Royal College of Psychiatrists explained in a book called 'Drug Scenes' that drug related crime was lower in the UK than in America for the following reasons:

'When comparison is made with the United States it is a striking feature of the British scene that on the whole addicts here are not involved in serious crimes in order to support their drug habit. There may be several reasons for this relatively benign situation. Drugs on the UK black market are relatively cheap. The welfare system also contributes to the possibility of supporting a drug habit without resort to serious crime. Perhaps an important factor is that there has been no evidence so far in the United Kingdom that people who become involved in drug use come from a grossly deprived urban environment with a sub-culture of violence, or from alienated racial minorities.'

The signs are that the situation has changed since 1987 and that whilst levels of drug-related crime in the UK are nowhere near as great as those in America, they are rising. This may be related to an increase in the number of people who are severely deprived and feel they have little to lose by being involved in criminal activity. There is a debate in the UK about the causes of, and solutions to, the general rise in crime. This will increasingly include consideration of how drug-related crime can be cut. The solutions people propose are very different. On the one hand people are calling for the decriminalisation of drug use. On the other, people propose getting tough on drug users by increasing surveillance and sentences.

Question
'The police should spend more time prosecuting young people for use of drugs. Young people would then stay well clear of them.' What do you think?

SHOULD CANNABIS USE BE LEGALISED?

Cannabis is the most commonly used illegal drug in the UK. Some people would like to see the law changed so it was no longer an offence to use cannabis. For others, legalising cannabis would be a backward step that would lead to more drug problems.

Legalisation would put cannabis in a similar category to alcohol and cigarettes. There still could be laws regulating sales and use but it would not be illegal to use or supply cannabis.

Decriminalisation is slightly different and means it would not be an offence to have small quantities of cannabis for personal use but production and supply would still be illegal.

FOR AND AGAINST

These are some of the arguments put forward by people who would like to see cannabis legalised:

For: Cannabis is a relatively safe drug. You cannot become physically dependent on cannabis or have a fatal overdose using it.

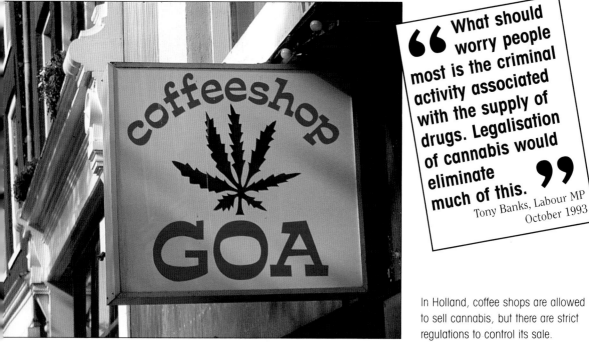

> **What should worry people most is the criminal activity associated with the supply of drugs. Legalisation of cannabis would eliminate much of this.**
> Tony Banks, Labour MP
> October 1993

In Holland, coffee shops are allowed to sell cannabis, but there are strict regulations to control its sale.

Chapter 7

For: Society is inconsistent if it allows alcohol and tobacco use but bans cannabis.

For: The fact that so many, and increasing numbers of, people use cannabis brings the law into disrepute. Laws are no longer workable if so many people break them and respect for the law diminishes.

For: The fact that cannabis is illegal causes all sorts of problems. Many people get a criminal record just for smoking cannabis. It wastes a tremendous amount of police, court and prison time which could be better spent on tackling serious crime.

For: Keeping cannabis illegal encourages large-scale drug dealers and associated crime and

> **When I talk about legalisation I am talking about the need for recognition that people use cannabis and that punishment is not the solution to the problem. We need to move away from enforcement and look at education and other approaches to try to influence people in the same way that we do with drink and cigarettes.**
>
> Midlands Police Chief Constable, June 1994

violence. It helps keep the black market going. The dealers may also deal in other illegal drugs which are more dangerous, and vulnerable youngsters are more likely to come into contact with drugs like cocaine and heroin.

For: Legalising cannabis would mean more control over its use. Price, strength and quality could be controlled. It could be taxed and the revenue could be put to needy causes. By making cannabis legal (and distinguishing between cannabis and more dangerous drugs like heroin and cocaine) the authorities would have much more credibility with young people.

For: Legalisation would not necessarily lead to more use of cannabis. When cannabis was decriminalised in Holland, research showed

that there was not an increase in use. We could still have controls over sales, making sure young people could not have easy access

> **Legalising cannabis wouldn't do any harm to anybody. We should be concentrating on the serious business of heroin and amphetamine.**
>
> Brian Hilliard, editor of Police Review magazine, June 1994

> **We have tried attacking the manufacturing facilities, the supply lines and the distribution networks but we are having no effect at all on the consumer market. There is no point in criminalising the user. They should be helped, not punished.**
>
> Ray Kendall, Police Chief Superintendent and British head of Interpol, 1994

to it, much as we do for alcohol and cigarettes. Spain, Switzerland, Italy and Germany are moving in a similar direction to Holland. Why not the UK?

For: If cannabis was legal to use we could have much more honest and open discussion about drugs. People who had any problems with its use would not be so reluctant to seek out advice and help.

For: Cannabis has many medical uses for conditions such as glaucoma (an eye disease), multiple sclerosis and for relieving the symptoms of AIDS and other illnesses. If it was legal it could be used more in medicine.

For: With a relatively harmless drug like cannabis the state should not interfere so much in its use. It should be up to individuals to make their own decisions about whether to use it or not.

THE CASE AGAINST

These are some of the arguments put forward by people who are against the legalisation of cannabis:

Against: Cannabis can be a dangerous drug. Any drug can be dangerous to the body and we need more research into its effects. We know smoking cannabis can damage the lungs like smoking cigarettes. Regular long-term use could be found to have lasting consequences. New stronger types of cannabis are being introduced which could be particularly dangerous.

Against: The fact that alcohol and cigarettes are legal to use is no excuse to allowing a free-for-all with cannabis.

> 66 I fear that if you make it acceptable for people to have drugs, they will find it acceptable and they will move from soft drugs to hard drugs, so I don't at all personally favour decriminalisation. 99
>
> John Major, Prime Minister, 1994

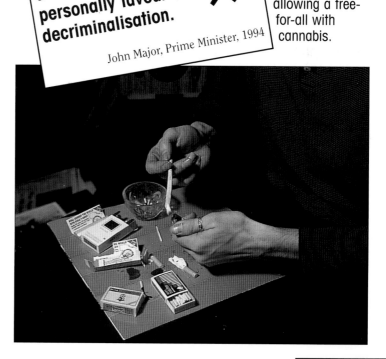

Lighting a 'joint', a hand-rolled cigarette containing cannabis

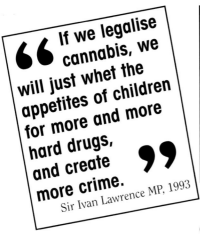

> **If we legalise cannabis, we will just whet the appetites of children for more and more hard drugs, and create more crime.**
> Sir Ivan Lawrence MP, 1993

> **Even if, heaven forbid, the authorities sold and taxed drugs, organised crime would undercut the price, intimidate and distort the market, while still controlling production... It is too soon to say we have failed....There is no place at this time for faint-hearted revisionists.**
> Graham Saltmarsh, National Crime Intelligence Centre, 1993

Legalising cannabis would be condoning its use and give out the wrong message to young people.

Against: More young people are using cannabis but they should be told to respect the law. The law is there to protect individuals and society. Anybody who uses cannabis knows the price of getting caught. They have to take responsibility for their own actions and suffer the consequences.

Against: If cannabis were legalised even more people would use it, including vulnerable, young people who might use it all the time.

Against: Cannabis use makes people lethargic, act foolishly and is very dangerous if people drive whilst 'stoned.'

Against: Legalising cannabis could be a slippery slope. Young people would get used to cannabis and then want to go on to try stronger and harder drugs. If cannabis were legalised what would happen next? Would drugs like heroin, cocaine and crack be legalised?

Against: Legalisation would have little impact on the drug barons and crime. The big dealers would merely concentrate on other drugs. And since cannabis can be grown in this country, legalisation may result in an even bigger illicit, homegrown market, undercutting legal supplies. There would still be little quality control.

Against: If cannabis is found to have some medical uses it could be prescribed without it being legalised. This is what currently happens with drugs like heroin and amphetamines.

Against: Legalising cannabis would be a step into the unknown. The consequences could be disastrous.

> **If you made cannabis more easily available you would put up the number of heavy users - and what we know about the risks of heavy use is very limited.**
> Professor Griffiths Edwards, National Addiction Centre

Question
You have read the main arguments for and against legalising cannabis. Where do you stand on the issue and why?

CANNABIS DECRIMINALISATION IN HOLLAND

Use of cannabis is not legal in Holland. Since 1976 it is no longer a crime to have up to 30 grammes of cannabis for personal use. The law still regards this as a 'misdemeanour' but this is a very minor offence and the police usually ignore it. This is what the Dutch mean by 'decriminalisation'. The reasons the Dutch decided to decriminalise cannabis use are similar to the reasons given on pages 42 and 43 in favour of legalisation.

In Holland cannabis is sold in coffee shops and in some youth centres where there are 'house' dealers. Growing, importing or dealing in large quantities of cannabis is still illegal. The police ignore supplies to coffee shops as long as it does not involve huge amounts or known criminals.

There are about 350 coffee shops in

A coffee shop in Amsterdam, Holland, where people can buy and smoke cannabis

Amsterdam and some in other cities in Holland. They are subject to a number of regulations. These include no sales of cannabis to juveniles, limits on advertising and no sales of other illegal drugs especially heroin, ecstasy, cocaine and crack. The police monitor coffee shops and some have been closed for breaking these rules.

Coffee shops are usually very relaxed and low key. They are often on side streets. Most do not sell alcohol but many serve cheap food, tea and coffee. They often have music, notice boards of local events, board games and newspapers to read. Coffee shops often sell different types of cannabis resin (hashish) and herbal cannabis (marijuana or grass) and sometimes have a menu describing what is on sale. They only sell relatively small quantities to people.

There is disagreement about the effect decriminalisation has had. A number of surveys have suggested that cannabis use has not increased in

> **We need further evidence and a much wider debate.**
>
> Keith Hellawell, Chief Constable of West Yorkshire

Amsterdam as a consequence. Other people point to the fact that many young tourists descend on Amsterdam because of the availability of cannabis.

A number of other countries are now following the Dutch example. Spain, Germany and Italy have recently changed their laws relating to cannabis so that it is no longer an offence for individuals to have small amounts in their possession. Strong opposition to changing the laws on cannabis comes from the American government through international forums such as the United Nations.

In the UK, the concern to reduce drug-related crime (see chapter 6) has also led to some senior police officers talking about decriminalising all drug use

by individuals and encouraging treatment rather than punishment for drug users. The idea is that people who are dependent on drugs would get their drugs from doctors, rather than buy them on the black market, and drug-related crime and violence would be greatly reduced. But the Home Secretary has recently increased fines for people who use cannabis. This met with much criticism from some senior judges, magistrates and police officers. At the same time more police forces have introduced a policy of cautioning people for use of cannabis rather than prosecuting them. Some people have said this is decriminalisation 'by the back door'. The debate is hotting up.

Question

'Alcohol is legal, acceptable, widely advertised and easily available. Cannabis is illegal. No wonder young people do not respect the law.' What do you think?

HOW SHOULD SCHOOLS DEAL WITH THE DRUGS ISSUE?

Surveys show that with the increase in numbers of young people using drugs every secondary school in the country will have its share of young drug users. This has led to an increase in 'drug incidents' where students have been caught with drugs in school. How should schools respond in such situations?

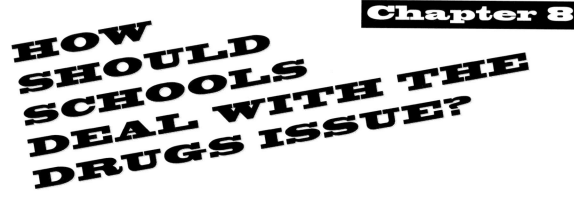

> ❝ Every secondary school has a drug or solvent abuse problem and so do many primary schools. There is no way that schools can ignore the issue. We need to tell the young the facts so they can make their own choices. ❞
>
> Peter Walker, head teacher and member of the Home Office Advisory Council on the Misuse of Drugs

DRUGS EDUCATION

A good school drugs education should be integrated into the Personal, Social and Health Education (PSE) curriculum rather than consist of the 'one off' lecture or video. It should address both legal and illegal drugs and be mainly led by teachers who have access to training and up-to-date teaching resources and drug information. Over the last few years new drugs education teaching packs have been published and many teachers have been trained in how best to deliver drugs education. Although the quantity and quality of drugs education varies greatly between different schools, on the whole the situation has greatly improved.

The teachers do not have to be 'drug experts'. Far more important are having teaching skills and developing relationships which enable students to discuss the drugs issue openly and honestly. Modern drug education resources utilise a range of teaching methods including quizzes, case studies, role play, brainstorming and small group discussion. Outside experts might be asked to contribute by speaking on specific topics.

Teachers often find that if they can create a trusting environment students sometimes talk about their own drug use and about use by people they know. This can raise difficult issues for teachers. Many introduce the ideas of confidentiality and ground rules with their groups. The idea is that people's confidentiality is respected so that students do not talk about each other's personal experiences outside class and that they

do not press each other to reveal personal information. The problem still arises for a teacher about what they should do if it is clear a student is having a problem with drugs. Should they tell the headteacher or the student's parents? How should they answer if asked about their own drug use?

Many schools are working towards a 'spiral curriculum' where drugs education features in every school year covering different aspects in more detail as students become older. Many focus on drugs such as alcohol, cigarettes and solvents in the early years and consider illegal drugs, the law and helping agencies later.

Most drug education programmes focus on secondary schools. A number of commentators have suggested that the work should begin in primary schools. The government is currently examining the possibility of drugs education in primary schools. What form this will take is, as yet, unclear.

Some schools have also developed drugs education work outside normal lesson time. This includes use of theatre companies, provision of information leaflets for students, notice boards with information about where to get help if it is needed, and so on.

Question

How good is the drugs education programme in your school? How could it be improved?

A teacher leads a drugs education section.

MANAGING DRUG INCIDENTS

If teachers know a student has been using or supplying drugs they do not have to inform the police or parents, even if this may be often the best thing to do. If teachers find an illegal drug in school they do not have to inform the police. It is legally permissible to dispose of the drug by, for example, flushing it down the toilet.

Schools cannot allow drug use or dealing on their premises. They need to make the rules, and punishments that follow from breaking the rules, clear to all students. If students are to be punished this needs to be handled sensibly. Some students have been immediately expelled on the basis of rumour or for failing to report fellow students who have brought drugs into school. If students use or deal in drugs in school it usually makes sense to suspend them for a short period whilst discussion of the situation takes place. Rushing into expulsions can mean mistakes are made, give out an uncaring message to other students and merely result in students being pushed from one school to another. The danger is that students who have problems will only be seen as a disciplinary matter and students will feel they cannot approach teachers if they have a problem with drugs in future.

INVOLVING POLICE AND PARENTS

Some schools always involve the police in such incidents. Others go to great lengths to avoid police involvement partly because they cannot be sure what steps the police might take. Developing a good relationship with local police is obviously important here.

Police responses to drug incidents in school can vary a lot in different areas. Faced with reports of small-scale cannabis dealing in school, some police officers have immediately carried out full-scale undercover operations whilst others have talked to the headteacher first and agreed together on what action should be taken.

Most schools will involve the student's parents but when and how the parents are contacted varies between schools. In exceptional cases – for example where there is evidence children will be physically abused if their parents find out – schools have not involved parents at all. It is usually best for schools to involve the students concerned in the decision about when parents are contacted and what they are told. Parents may be very shocked about hearing their children are involved with drugs and may be quite ignorant about drugs. Schools can have an important role in educating parents and helping them and their children deal with the situation sensibly.

Some schools have also developed good working relationships with Drug Agencies, sought their advice in such situations and, where appropriate, referred students for help. The danger here is that students are 'sent for counselling' even if they do not really have a problem with drugs and do not want to talk to drug workers about it.

WIDER INITIATIVES

Many schools are beginning to take the drugs issue seriously and are looking at ways of helping students and the wider community. As well as developing a good drugs education programme and handling drug incidents sensitively they are:

- Developing a school policy on drugs. Some schools have involved the whole school community in writing their policy, including teachers, other staff, school governors, parents and students.

- Developing links with drug agencies who can offer advice to teachers and help students if they have problems with drugs.

- Providing training courses for teachers. Some schools and Education

Question
'Teachers are the best people to teach drugs education to young people.' What do you think?

Authorities arrange drugs awareness training (covering facts about drugs, attitudes, patterns of drug use etc.) for all staff as well as more specialised training for staff who teach drugs education and handle drug incidents.

- Running parent and governor drugs awareness workshops to help educate adults, allay their fears and encourage them to talk to their children about the drugs issue. These workshops tend to go down very well with parents who attend. Some have been run with students and parents attending together and exchanging views.

Find out
'If a student brings a drug like cannabis into school they should be immediately expelled.' What do you think? Do other students and teachers agree with you?

Whilst some schools still find the drugs issue too difficult to address others are putting a lot of time and effort into it. Rather than thinking that tackling drugs education will give the school a bad name they believe they are taking a caring and understanding approach based on community concerns.

WHAT CAN BE DONE ABOUT DRUG USE?

There are four main ways in which the drugs issue can be addressed in society:

- **Prevention and education programmes** in schools, the media etc.
- **Treatment and helping services** for people who have problems with use of drugs.
- **Drug laws and policing** which try to limit the use and supply of drugs.
- **Controlling supplies of drugs coming into the country**
  Governments focus on all four areas, each to lesser or greater extent, to develop drug policies.

EDUCATION PROGRAMMES

Governments and health and education authorities can fund education programmes, mostly targeted at young people and parents, and carried out in schools or through the media. A key decision is whether to focus on primary prevention (trying to stop people using drugs in the first place) or harm reduction. Most programmes have been based on primary prevention despite the fact that evaluations show this approach to be ineffective (see chapter 5).

In addition some local drug agencies and health projects have produced their own education and information materials. Some of the leaflets which have had a harm reduction message have caused considerable controversy.

Most people agree that young people and adults need access to up-to-date and accurate information about drugs and related issues. A lot of money has gone into such work in the last few years. Whether it has been wisely spent and whether it has had a significant impact on knowledge about drugs and patterns of drug use are open to question.

TREATMENT AND HELPING SERVICES

As more people have begun to use drugs, more treatment and helping services have become available. These include:

- **Family doctors** who may be able to provide counselling, prescribe substitute drugs (such as methadone to heroin users) and refer drug users to other services.

- **Drug advice and counselling services** which can provide counselling, information and advice, clean syringes and referral to other services and sometimes prescribe substitute drugs.

- **Hospital-based drug services** which specialise in 'detoxification' for people who are dependent on drugs like heroin.

- **Specialist needle exchange schemes** which offer free, clean injecting equipment to drug injectors, health advice and access to other services. These schemes grew in response to the danger of contracting HIV – the virus that leads to AIDS – through sharing injecting equipment.

- **Residential rehabilitation centres** where people with long-term drug problems can go for a period of time to learn to live without drugs.

- **Self-help groups** for drug users, parents and families in which people can support each other.

In some areas of the country there is a full range of services. In other areas very little help exists. But are the services that do exist successful? People who criticise the services ask questions such as:

- Are needle exchanges successful in stopping sharing of injecting equipment or do they actually encourage people to carry on injecting drugs?

- Should dependent heroin users be prescribed drugs and if so which drugs and on what basis?

- Are drug-helping services right for the young people who use drugs other than heroin?

- What should be done about drug use in prisons?

Question
A needle exchange is to be set up on the street where you live. Would you support it or object to it?

DRUG LAWS AND POLICING

Some countries, particularly the USA, have tried to tackle the drugs problem by introducing harsher laws and increasing police powers and surveillance. Unfortunately this seems to have led to an increase in drug-related violence, filled the prisons to breaking point and led to a loss of civil liberties and freedoms for the population at large.

In New York it was made illegal for helping agencies to give out clean injecting equipment. Rather than resulting in a decrease in drug use this has contributed to the enormous number of injecting drug users who have died of AIDS and who have HIV. (An estimated 100,000 drug injectors have HIV and more than 5,000 have died of AIDS in New York).

The American government also promoted drug testing of workers by awarding contracts to companies who tested their employees. Testing has led to many people losing their jobs for using drugs, even if they performed their work well. None of these harsh measures have reduced drug problems and some experts suggest they may have created more problems than previously existed.

There is a trend in the UK towards 'compulsory treatment' whereby drug offenders can avoid prison or heavy fines if they agree to be treated for their drug problem. The difficulty here is that people can only usually start to deal with their drug problems if they want to themselves rather than being forced to do so.

Question
Do you think school students or employees should be drug tested?

There have been changes in the law relating to alcohol and cigarettes in recent years. The licensing laws have changed allowing pubs to open for longer hours. The police have been given greater powers to stop and breathalyse drivers and some cities have introduced by-laws banning the drinking of alcohol on the streets. Whilst the main laws about cigarette sales have remained the same many public places and workplaces have become no-smoking areas, with fines for people who break the rules.

STEMMING THE SUPPLY OF DRUGS

The UK government is involved, with other governments, in attempting to stop the raw ingredients from which drugs are made being grown in Third World countries. In particular, opium (from which heroin is made) and coca (from which cocaine and crack are made) are targeted. Some programmes have tried to encourage farmers to grow other, non-drug crops. But poor Third World farmers have often found substitute crops do not bring in as much money. Different countries have different drug policies. Some countries, such as Thailand, have very harsh laws such as the death penalty for drug trafficking and have few education or treatment programmes. The American approach includes severe penalties for use and supply of drugs and wide-ranging police powers to intercept supplies but also uses a range of treatment services

Customs officers seize heroin worth £30 million on its way into Britain.

and high-profile prevention campaigns. The Netherlands model relies more on treatment and helping services and less on the law to tackle drug problems. They emphasise tackling drugs as a health rather than a legal/criminal issue and their example is increasingly followed in other European countries.

In order to develop sensible policies to deal with drugs, other issues in society must be taken into account. We know that if people have a decent standard of living and see a good future for themselves they are less likely to use drugs in a heavy or chaotic way. Reducing drug problems may have as much to do with reducing poverty and inequality in society as it has to do with good drugs education and helping services and sensible laws and policing.

WHAT CAN YOUNG PEOPLE DO ABOUT DRUG USE?

There are many ways that young people can be active in doing something positive about drug use.

1 Inform yourself further. Look at some of the books listed on page 60. Contact local and national organisations for more information about drugs.

2 Talk to other people - friends, your parents, teachers, police officers etc. - about drug use. It is a complex issue. The more people who talk openly about drugs and share views the better.

3 Help develop realistic drugs education and information work. You might get involved with staff and other students in school or at a local youth or community centre. You could help write, produce and distribute leaflets, help organise discussion sessions or get involved in making decisions about what the school does about drugs.

4 Help educate your parents. Often young people know more about drugs than their parents. Help your parents by talking to them, explaining things to them, showing them this book or some good drug information leaflets.

5 Help friends and acquaintances who have a problem with drugs. Often when people are using drugs heavily or get into problems their friends turn their backs on them. Make sure you don't. Offer to help and be prepared to listen to them. You might need their help one day.

Question
If you were Prime Minister, what changes would you make in drug policy and why?

Question
'Drug problems have more to do with poverty than drugs themselves.' What do you think?

DRUGS: THE FACTS

This section gives some information about commonly used drugs. If you wish to find out more about any of the drugs see **Further Reading** (page 60). If you wish to know more about the laws controlling drugs use see chapter 6 of this book. Each of the descriptions of drugs below includes some of the street names. These are only a selection - street names tend to vary over time and between different places.

ALCOHOL is, apart from caffeine, the most commonly used drug in the UK.
Effects: Alcohol is a depressant drug which slows down body functioning. Small amounts make people less inhibited and more relaxed. Larger amounts lead to slurred speech and poor co-ordination. Huge amounts can lead to loss of consciousness. Alcohol increases the likelihood of all sorts of accidents. A huge dose can lead to fatal overdose. It is associated with violent behaviour and can make practising safer sex more difficult. Alcohol can be very dangerous mixed with other downer drugs like heroin or tranquillisers. Regular heavy use leads to physical dependence and tolerance as well as possible liver, heart, stomach and brain damage.
The law: It is illegal for an under 5 to drink alcohol. It is legal for over 5s to drink alcohol away from licensed premises. The law allows 14-year-olds to go into pubs but not drink alcohol. A 16-year-old can purchase and drink alcohol (but not spirits) in a pub if they are having a meal. 18-year-olds can purchase alcohol and drink in pubs without having a meal. A few areas have laws banning use of alcohol on city streets.

AMPHETAMINE (speed, sulphate, whizz) is a synthetic stimulant drug. It mostly comes in powder form but sometimes as a tablet. It can be sniffed or swallowed in a drink but is also sometimes injected.
Effects: Amphetamine increases energy, keeps people awake and makes them less hungry. After using amphetamine people often feel very tired, depressed and hungry. Use can also make people feel very anxious and disturb regular sleep, diet and work patterns. Amphetamine often has a load of rubbish mixed in with it and this can itself be dangerous. Regular, heavy use can lead to depression and paranoia - thinking everyone is getting at you. Some people also become very aggressive and have violent mood changes. Regular use can lead to psychological dependence where people feel they can't do without it. Injecting can lead to additional dangers, including HIV if injecting equipment is shared.
The law: Amphetamine is illegal to possess without a prescription or supply to other people.

ANABOLIC STEROIDS are similar to the hormones in the body which regulate growth and development. They can be made from natural or synthetic sources. Common trade names include Dianabol, Durabolin, Nadrolone and Stanozolol. They are usually swallowed as pills but sometimes injected.
Effects: Steroids increase muscle size and body weight. They often make people more aggressive and competitive and more able to perform strenuous physical activity. Regular use can damage the liver and lead to water retention, high blood pressure, male fertility problems, 'male' characteristics in women and growth problems amongst young people. Some users come to feel they cannot perform well without them. Regular use has also been connected with violent behaviour. Injecting carries additional risks including HIV if injecting equipment is shared. **The law:** It is not illegal to use steroids but it is an offence to supply them to other people. The Government is considering changing the law.

BARBITURATES (barbs, barbies, bullets, devils, nembies, sleepers) are man-made drugs made for medical use to treat depression and anxiety and as sleeping tablets.
Effects: They are very strong sedative, downer drugs. In small doses they give a relaxing effect. With large doses people tend to slur their speech, lose co-ordination and possibly fall asleep. They are very easy to fatally overdose on. Physical

dependence and tolerance (needing a larger dose to get the same effect) can develop quickly. Dependent users who stop abruptly can experience fits. Barbiturates are sometimes injected bringing additional risks, including HIV if injecting equipment is shared.

The law: They are illegal to possess (without a prescription) or to supply to other people.

CAFFEINE is the most commonly used drug in the UK. It is found in tea, coffee, cocoa, some chocolate and many soft drinks.

Effects: Caffeine is a mild stimulant and combats drowsiness and tiredness. It can help people concentrate and increases heart rate and blood pressure. It also makes people urinate more often. High doses can lead to headaches and feeling irritable. Regular, high doses usually result in dependence. People taking 6-8 cups of tea or coffee a day often find it difficult to stop and have withdrawal symptoms (feeling tired, headaches, irritability etc.) if they try. Heavy, long term use may increase the risk of peptic ulcers, kidney, bladder and heart disease and contribute to blood pressure problems.

The law: Caffeine is not illegal.

CANNABIS (blow, bush, dope, draw, ganga, grass, hash, marijuana, pot, sensi, skunk, sputnik, wacky backy, weed and many other names) comes from the Cannabis sativa plant which is grown all over the world. It comes in three forms: herbal/ grass form from the leaf, resin or block form or a black oil. It is usually smoked in a 'joint', with or without tobacco, but can be smoked in pipes, eaten or cooked with. Cannabis is by far the most widely used illegal drug in the UK. It is not usually prescribed in this country but has a number of medical uses.

Effects: The effects of using cannabis vary on the user's mood and expectations. People often feel relaxed, talkative and giggly and find colour and sound enhanced. Large doses can make people anxious especially if they are already edgy. Feelings of being hungry and forgetful are common. There is no danger of physical dependence or overdose. Psychological dependence may develop in some people who feel they can only relax when stoned. Cannabis affects co-ordination and increases the risks of accidents, especially when driving. It also lowers inhibitions, making unsafe sex more likely. Regular high doses may lead to lethargy, paranoia and anxiety and can damage the lungs. This may be more common with stronger types of cannabis like sensimilla - a strong herbal form.

The law: Cannabis is illegal to possess or supply to other people.

COCAINE (C, charlie, coke, snow, white) and crack (base, freebase, gravel, ice, rock, wash) are strong, short-lived, stimulant drugs made from the coca shrub which grows in South America. Cocaine is a powder and usually sniffed up the nose but sometimes prepared for injection. Crack is a crystalline form of cocaine which is usually smoked.

Effects: Although not regarded as drugs that cause physical dependence users may get into a pattern of regular use to maintain feelings of energy and power and avoid feeling low. The strong stimulant effect can be dangerous for people with blood pressure or heart problems. Regular users may find they get very run down, depressed and paranoid if they stop using.

The law: Cocaine and crack are illegal to possess or supply to other people.

ECSTASY (E, echoes, XTC, love doves, MDMA and many other names) is a synthetic drug that combines stimulant and hallucinogenic effects. It usually comes in a tablet or capsule form.

Effects: It gives a 'rush' of energy, keeping people awake and active. People say this is usually followed by feelings of calmness, closeness to other people and greater awareness of surroundings, colours and sounds. High doses can make people feel very panicky. Regular use can lead to sleep problems, lethargy and depression. Little is yet known about the effects on the body of long term use. Tablets sold as ecstasy may have other ingredients mixed in with them, and may not even be ecstasy at all. Taking the drug and taking part in non-stop

dancing has lead to death from overheating and dehydration. Rest, and plenty of water to drink, can help to avoid this danger. Ecstasy can also be dangerous to people with heart or blood pressure problems.
The law: Ecstasy is illegal to possess or supply to other people.

HEROIN (gear, H, harry, horse, jack, junk, scat, skag, smack) is a powder made from the opium poppy. There are also many other naturally occurring and synthetic heroin-type drugs such as codeine, diconal, methadone, morphine, opium, palfium, pethidine and temegesic. Heroin is a strong painkiller and medically prescribed for terminally ill cancer patients. Illicit users sometimes smoke or sniff it but it is the most commonly injected illegal drug in the UK. Street users who seek treatment are often prescribed methadone in syrup form as a substitute.
Effects: It slows people down giving them a feeling of warmth and detachment. Low doses tend to reduce anxiety and block emotional pain. Higher doses lead to drowsiness. With regular use physical dependence and tolerance (taking more to get an effect) develop. Overdose is a real risk and can result in coma or death. Street heroin is mixed with rubbish and this, in itself, increases the dangers. Injecting can lead to additional health problems and HIV, if injecting equipment is shared.
The law: Heroin is illegal to

possess (without a prescription) or supply to other people.

LSD (A, acid, dots, star, tab, trips and many other names depending on the pictures on the blotters) is a powerful hallucinogenic drug made from a fungus which grows on rye grass. Only tiny amounts are needed to get an effect. It is usually dropped on to paper squares or 'blotters' but occasionally comes as a pill or capsule.
Effects: LSD use results in a 'trip' lasting anything up to 12 hours. Visual and sound distortions, intensified colours and changes in the sense of time and place are common. However, a 'bad trip' can be very disturbing. People may feel very anxious and paranoid and feel everyone and everything is threatening them. They may think they are going mad and may do dangerous things whilst tripping. People who are very anxious or have mental health problems may find LSD particularly disturbing. Accidents are more likely as concentrating is difficult. It is also difficult to know how strong a dose you are taking. LSD does not lead to physical dependence or fatal overdose. In fact it is ineffective if used too often. There is no known physical damage to the body but some users get 'flashbacks'. This is where they re-experience a 'trip' some time afterwards. This can be very disturbing, especially if people are not aware that it can happen.

The law: LSD is illegal to possess or supply to others.

MAGIC MUSHROOMS (liberties, mushies, psilocybe) are small bell shaped mushrooms which grow wild all over the country in early autumn. They are usually eaten raw. 20-30 is regarded as a full dose.
Effects: They have hallucinogenic effects similar to LSD (see above). One danger is picking the wrong type. Some mushrooms are poisonous. Users sometimes get a stomach ache from using them. Feeling sick is also common.
The law: The law on magic mushrooms is complicated. There is no law against picking them and eating them raw. However, if they are dried out and stored, cooked with or made into a tea they become illegal to posses or supply.

POPPERS (Amyl, butyl, liquid gold, locker room, nitrites, ram, rush, snapper, stag, stud, thrust, TNT and other brand names) are a gold coloured liquid. They come in a small bottle or sometimes in small glass 'vials' which are popped open.
Effects: The vapours are inhaled through the nose and/ or mouth. They give a quick rushing feeling and people often feel time is being slowed down. Loss of balance, headache and nausea are common. Poppers are seen by some people as aphrodisiacs enhancing sexual pleasure. Users sometimes lose consciousness, especially if they are dancing. The sudden increase in heart rate means

they are particularly dangerous to people with heart or blood pressure problems. Regular use can result in skin problems. There have been a few fatalities when people have drunk, rather than sniffed, poppers. Use does not lead to physical dependence and there is no definite evidence of health damage from long term use.

The law: Poppers are not illegal.

SOLVENTS include many glues, butane gas, many aerosols, petrol, dry cleaning fluids, typewriter correction fluids, nail varnish remover etc. Many households are crammed full of sniffable products.

Effects: The effect of solvents come on fast but do not last long. It has been described as a bit like becoming drunk very quickly. People tend to feel light headed and dreamy. Others may feel sick and drowsy. When it wears off users often experience a hangover. Solvent use increases the risks of accidents especially when used in dangerous places like river banks or near roads. Every year in the UK about 150 youngsters die using solvents and some are first time users. Use can lead to loss of consciousness and if people choke on their own vomit they can die. Some users have suffocated by placing a large plastic bag in which to sniff solvents over their head. Squirting gases or aerosols straight down the throat has also led to deaths from heart failure or freezing the airways. Long term heavy use has been

associated with brain, kidney and liver damage but this is very rare. Physical dependence does not result from solvent use but some youngsters get into a pattern of using heavily every day.

The law: It is not illegal to use solvents. It is illegal for a shopkeeper to sell solvents to someone they know is under 18 and will use the solvents to get high.

TOBACCO contains the drug nicotine which is a mild stimulant. Tobacco can be chewed in the mouth or sniffed up the nose as snuff but more often is smoked as cigarettes, cigars or in pipes.

Effects: Effects of smoking are quick. Heart rate and blood pressure go up. Regular users often say they feel less anxious and that it combats boredom and helps concentration. Some say it makes them less hungry. Tolerance develops very quickly in smokers so more cigarettes are smoked to get an effect. Most smokers quickly become dependent and feel restless, irritable and depressed if they try to stop. Very few people manage to be only occasional smokers. Regular use greatly increases the risk of various cancers, heart problems, bronchitis, ulcers etc. Every year in the UK over 100,000 people die prematurely due to the effects of smoking tobacco. There is also the risk from 'passive smoking' - the effect of smoking on non smokers who have to inhale tobacco smoke.

This causes several hundred deaths a year and has been associated with chest and asthma problems, especially in children.

The law: It is not illegal to smoke tobacco products. It is illegal for shopkeepers to sell tobacco products to children they know to be under 16 years of age.

TRANQUILLISERS (tranx, benzodiazipines) include drugs like ativan, librium, mogadon, temazepam and valium. They are one of the most commonly prescribed medical drugs in the UK. They are used to treat anxiety, depression, insomnia, epilepsy and other things.

Effects: They are depressant drugs which slow people down and make them less anxious. They can also make people lethargic, drowsy and forgetful. They tend to shut out feelings. They are relatively easy to become dependent on and many people are hooked on long term repeat prescriptions from their doctor. If people are hooked on them, trying to stop can be very difficult and lead to anxiety, panic, headaches, nausea and confusion. There have also been many fatal overdoses especially when they are taken in combination with alcohol.

The law: They are covered under the Misuse of Drugs Act but the possession offence is waved. This means it is not illegal to possess them without a prescription. However, it is illegal to supply them to other people.

HELPLINE

National Organisations

HEALTHWISE 9 Slater Street, Liverpool L1 4BW. Tel. 0151 707 2262. Publish a range of drugs education packs, computer games and card games for use with young people.

ISDD (Institute for the Study of Drug Dependence) Waterbridge House, 32-36 Loman Street, London SE1 OEE. Tel. 0171 928 1211. The main source of up to date drugs information in the UK. Produce pamphlets and reports on drugs and 'Druglink' magazine. Also have an excellent library service.

NATIONAL DRUGS HELPLINE Tel. 0800 776600 Free, confidential advice 24 hours a day.

RELEASE 388 Old Street, London EC1V 9LT. Tel. 0171 729 9904 or 0171 603 8654 out of hours. Information and advice about legal aspects of drug use.

SCODA (Standing Conference on Drug Abuse) Waterbridge House, 32-36 Loman Street, London SE1 OEE. Tel. 0171 928 9500. Information about drugs and drug advice and helping services. They keep an up to date list of drug services in different areas.

Local organisations

There should be a range of organisations in your area which can help you with information or advice about drugs or help if you, or a friend, ever had a problem with drugs.

These organisations should include:

• A Drugs Advice and Counselling Service
• A Health Promotion Unit (which comes under the Health Authority)
• A Health Education Co-ordinator (who comes under the council Education Department)

To find out which organisations exist in your area contact your Health Authority or Education Department, look in the phone book under 'DRUGS' or ask at a Citizen's Advice Bureau. If you come unstuck try ringing the National Drugs Helpline (telephone number above) and they may be able to help.

IN AUSTRALIA

Alcohol and Drug Information Service in your state or territory.
New South Wales (02) 331 2111 (outside Sydney) 1800 422 599
Victoria (03 9416 1818 (ouside Melbourne) 1800 136 385
Queensland (07) 3236 2414 (outside Brisbane) 1800 177 833

South Australia 13 1340
Western Australia (09) 421 1900 (outside Perth) 1800 198 024
Tasmania (002) 784 111 or 1800 811 994
ACT (06) 205 4545
Northern Territory (089) 818 030 or 1800 629 683

The Australian Drug Foundation is a non-government, non-profit organisation committed to reducing the harm caused by alcohol and drug use. Pamphlets, books, videos and other resources are available from the Foundation. The foundation also runs a wide range of programmes aimed at preventing drug problems in the community.

Contact: 1800 069 700

FURTHER READING

Listed below are a range of books about drug use. Some are available from good bookshops. They should all be available through a good public library.

V. Berridge and G. Edwards **Opium and the people**, Yale 1987. Paperback book describing opium, cannabis and cocaine use in 19th century Britain.

J. Cohen and J. Kay **Taking Drugs Seriously - A Parent's Guide to Young People's Drug Use**, Thorsons 1994. Paperback book for parents which will also be of interest to young people. It includes exercises about drugs parents and young people can do together.

J. Davis and N. Coggans **The Facts about Adolescent Drug Abuse**, Cassell 1991. Paperback book covering what we mean by drugs and drug problems, extent of use of drugs, drugs education etc.

G. Edwards, A. Arif and J. Jaffe eds. **Drug Use and Misuse - Cultural Perspectives**, Croom Helm 1983. Series of articles about drug use in different countries and cultures.

M. Gossop **Living with Drugs**, Ashgate 1993. Paperback book covering history and sociology of drug use.

B. Inglis **The Forbidden Game - A Social History of Drugs**, Hodder and Stoughton 1975. A history of drug use, attitudes and controls from the earliest times to the 20th century.

ISDD **Drug Abuse Briefing** 1994. Detailed pamphlet on the effects, risks, legality of different drugs. Includes colour photos of drugs.

M. Plant and M. Plant **Risk Takers: Alcohol, Drugs, Sex and Youth**, Routledge 1992. Paperback book covering causes of drug use, extent of use, drug related harm and drugs education and prevention.

P. Robson **Forbidden Drugs**, Oxford University Press 1994. Paperback giving detailed information about the use of illegal drugs.

Royal College of Psychiatrists **Drug Scenes**, Gaskell 1987. Paperback covering drug terms, information about drugs, prevention and treatment.

D. Stockley **Drug Warning**, Optima 1992. Paperback giving facts about different drugs. Many colour photos.

A. Tyler **Street Drugs**, Hodder and Stoughton 1995. Paperback covering history and effects of different drugs.